+ BEGINNING PIANO SOLO +

BROADWAY FAVORITES

ISBN 978-1-5400-6748-7

HAL•LEONARD®

Visit Hal Leonard Online at
www.halleonard.com

Contact us:
Hal Leonard
7777 West Bluemound Road
Milwaukee, WI 53213
Email: info@halleonard.com

In Europe, contact:
Hal Leonard Europe Limited
42 Wigmore Street
Marylebone, London, W1U 2RN
Email: info@halleonardeurope.com

In Australia, contact:
Hal Leonard Australia Pty. Ltd.
4 Lentara Court
Cheltenham, Victoria, 3192 Australia
Email: info@halleonard.com.au

CONTENTS

ANY DREAM WILL DO

from JOSEPH AND THE AMAZING TECHNICOLOR® DREAMCOAT

Music by ANDREW LLOYD WEBBER
Lyrics by TIM RICE

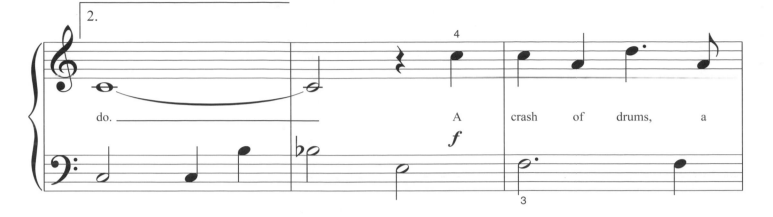

do. _____ A crash of drums, a

flash of light, my gold - en coat flew out of sight. The

col - ors fad - ed in - to dark - ness, I was left a -

lone. _____ May I re - turn

to the be - gin - ning, the light is dim - ming,

and the dream is, too. The world and I,

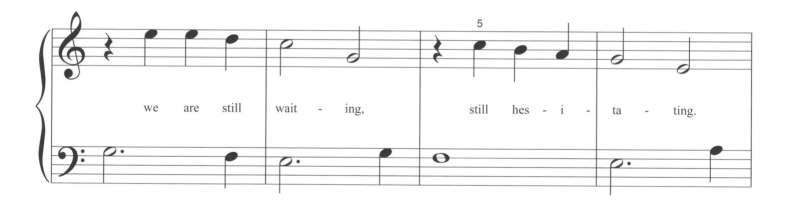

we are still wait - ing, still hes - i - ta - ting.

An - y dream will do. _____

CONSIDER YOURSELF

from the Broadway Musical OLIVER!

Words and Music by
LIONEL BART

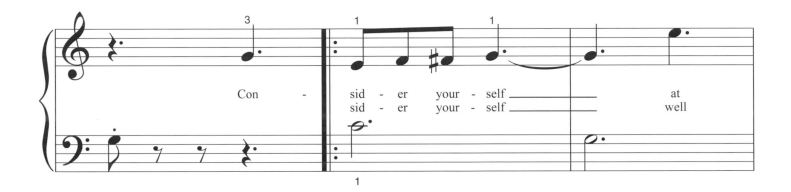

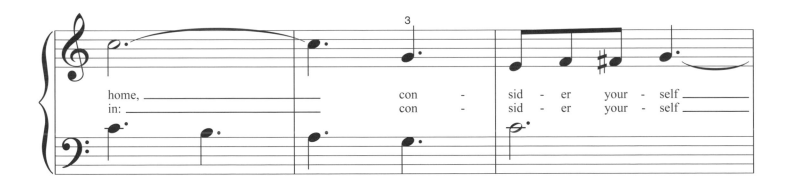

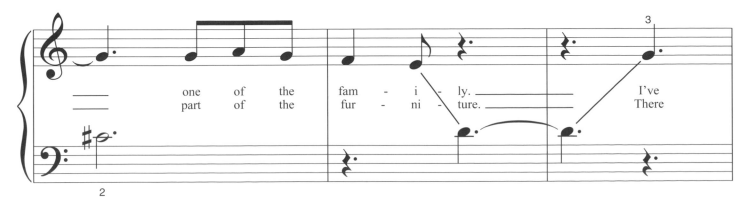

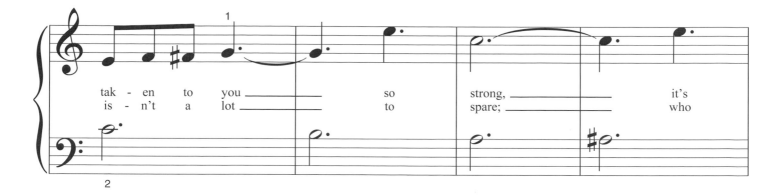

tak - en to you ____ so strong, ____ it's
is - n't a lot ____ to spare; ____ who

clear
cares? we're
What - ev - er we've got we
go - ing to get a - long! Con -

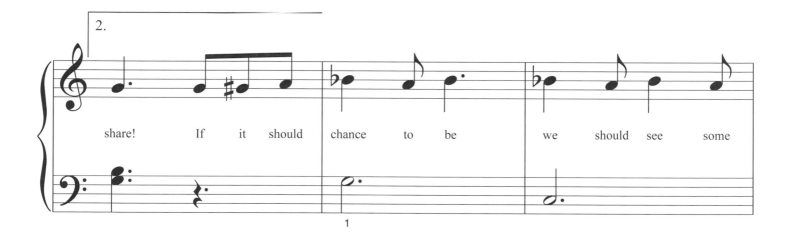

share! If it should chance to be we should see some

hard - er days, ____ emp - ty lard - er days, ____

_____ why grouse? _____ Al - ways a chance we'll meet

some - bod - y to foot the bill, _____ then the

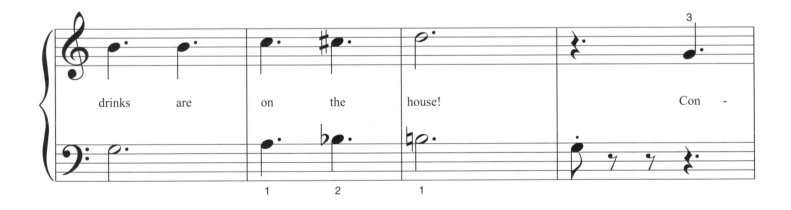

drinks are on the house! Con -

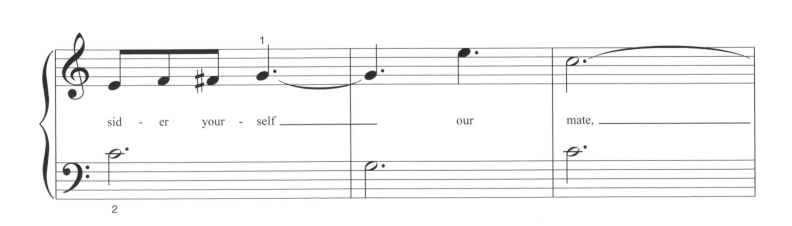

sid - er your - self _____ our mate, _____

we don't want to have ____ no fuss ____

____ for af - ter some con - sid - er - a - tion,

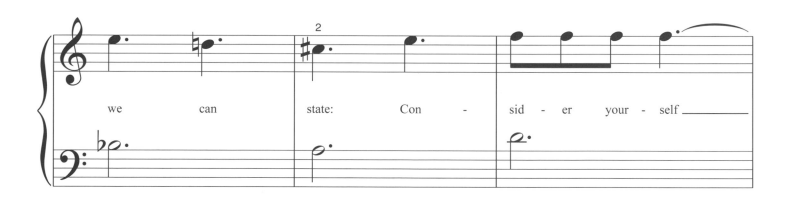

we can state: Con - sid - er your - self ____

____ one of us.

GREEN EGGS AND HAM

from SEUSSICAL THE MUSICAL

Words by LYNN AHRENS
and Dr. SEUSS
Music by STEPHEN FLAHERTY

Moderately fast

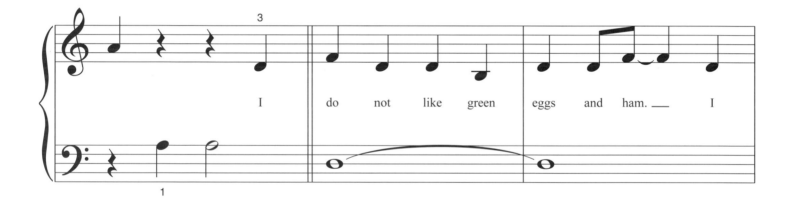

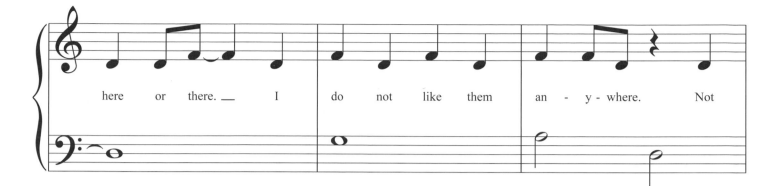

here or there. ___ I do not like them an - y - where. Not

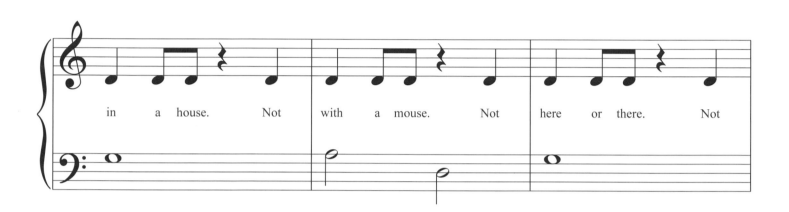

in a house. Not with a mouse. Not here or there. Not

an - y - where. I do not like green eggs and ham. I

do not like them Sam I Am! Could ___ you? Would you?

With a goat? Could you? Would you? On a boat? Could

you? Would you? In the rain? Could you? Would you?

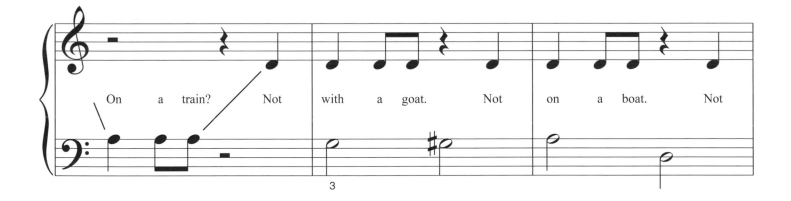

On a train? Not with a goat. Not on a boat. Not

3

in the rain. Not on a train. Not in a house. Not

I KNOW THINGS NOW

from INTO THE WOODS

Words and Music by
STEPHEN SONDHEIM

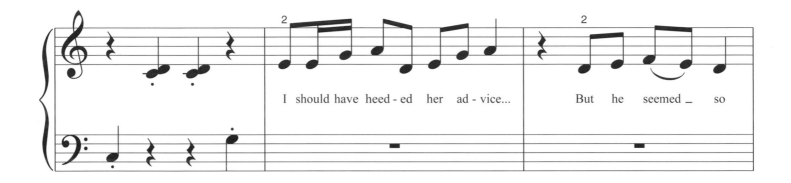

15

plore.   They were   off   my   path,   so   I   nev - er   had   dared.   I   had
fore: Do   not   put   your   faith   in   a   cape   and   a   hood,   they   will

been   so   care - ful   you   the   nev - er   had   cared.   And   he
not   so   pro - tect   you   the   way   that   they   should.   And   take

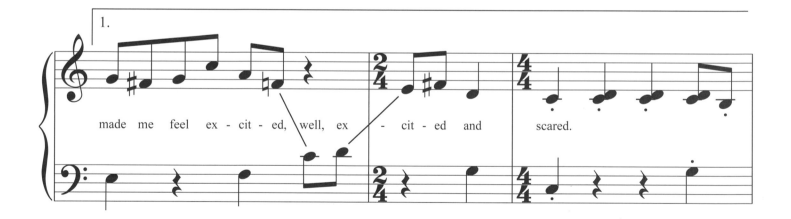

1.

made   me   feel   ex - cit - ed,   well,   ex -   cit - ed   and   scared.

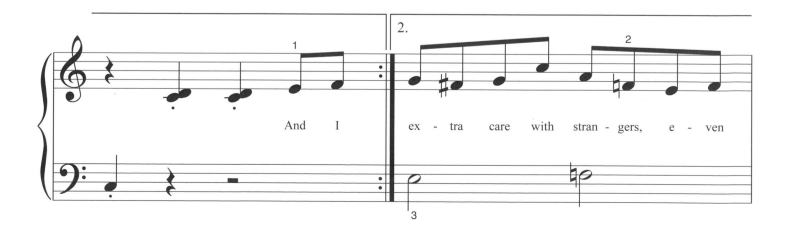

2.

And   I   ex - tra   care   with   stran - gers,   e - ven

flow - ers have their dan - gers. And though scar - y is ex - cit - ing, nice is dif - f'rent than

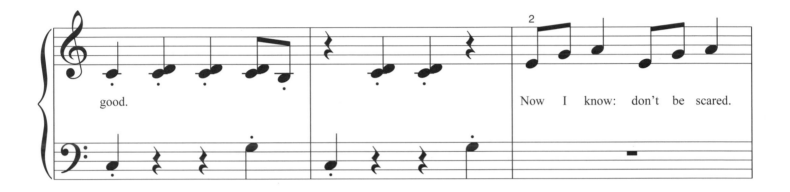

good. Now I know: don't be scared.

Gran - ny is right, just be pre - pared. Is - n't it nice to know a lot!

And a lit - tle bit not...

mp

SINGIN' IN THE RAIN

from SINGIN' IN THE RAIN

Lyric by ARTHUR FREED
Music by NACIO HERB BROWN

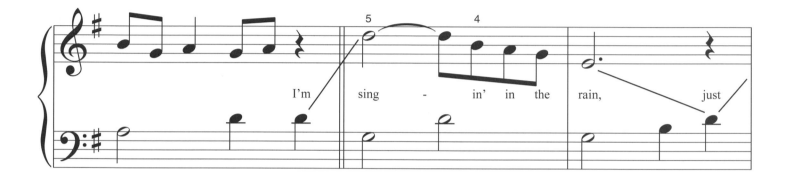

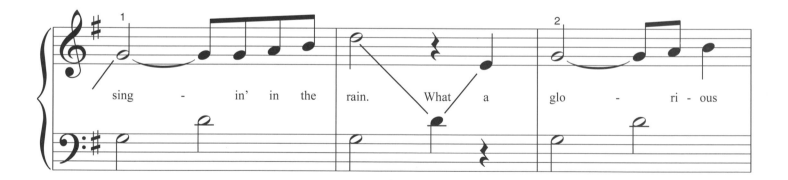

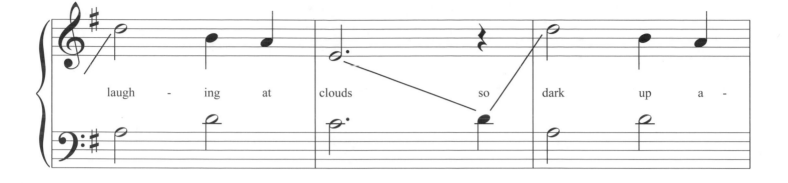

laugh - ing at clouds so dark up a -

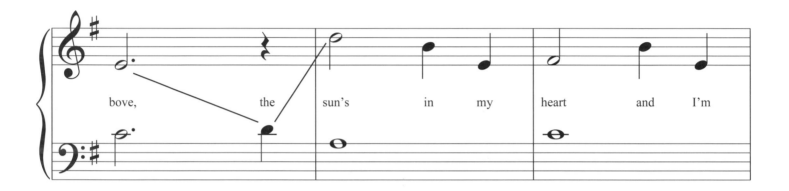

bove, the sun's in my heart and I'm

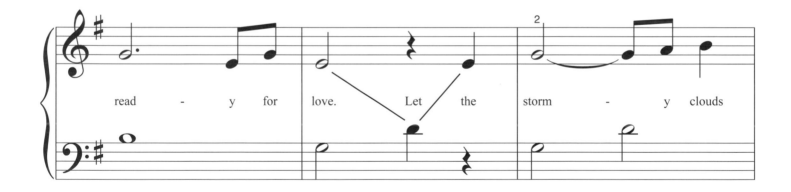

read - y for love. Let the storm - y clouds

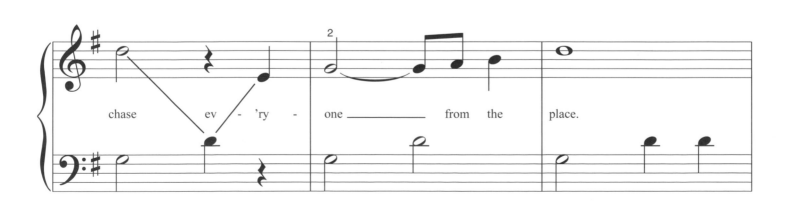

chase ev - 'ry - one _____ from the place.

Come on _____ with the rain, I've a smile on my

face. I'll walk down the lane with a

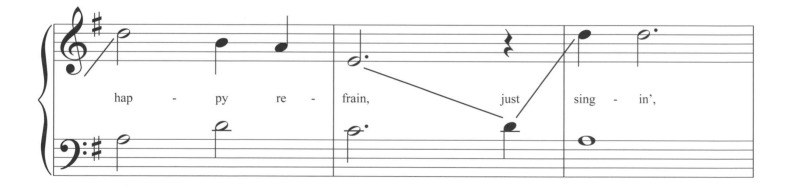

hap - py re - frain, just sing - in',

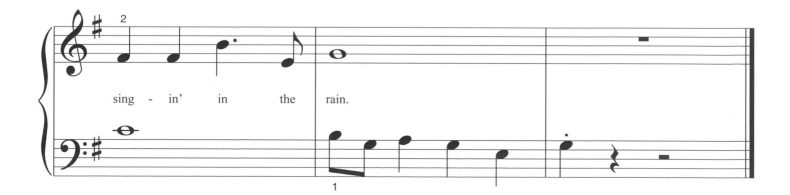

sing - in' in the rain.

I WHISTLE A HAPPY TUNE

from THE KING AND I

Lyrics by OSCAR HAMMERSTEIN II
Music by RICHARD RODGERS

When - ev - er I feel a - fraid, I hold my head e -
shiv - er - ing in my shoes, I strike a care - less

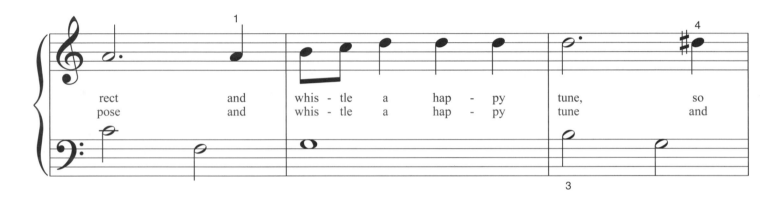

rect and whis - tle a hap - py tune, so
pose and whis - tle a hap - py tune and

no one will sus - pect I'm a - fraid.
no one ev - er

While knows I'm a - fraid.

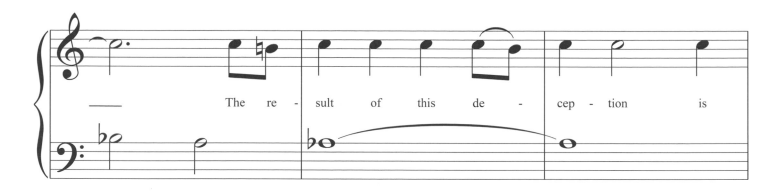

The re - sult of this de - cep - tion is

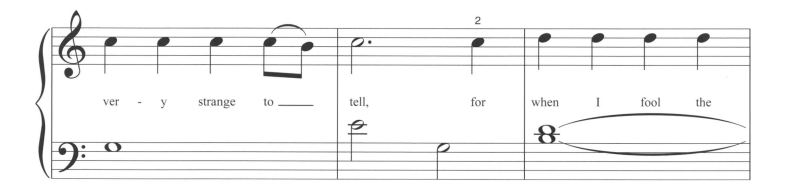

ver - y strange to _____ tell, for when I fool the

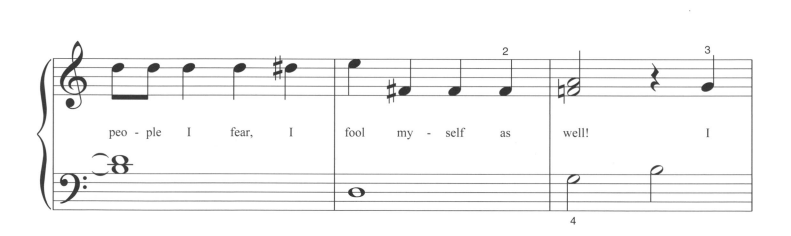

peo - ple I fear, I fool my - self as well! I

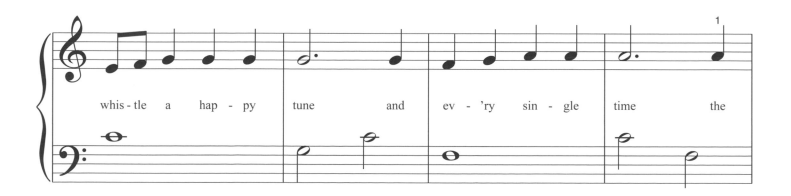

whis - tle a hap - py tune and ev - 'ry sin - gle time the

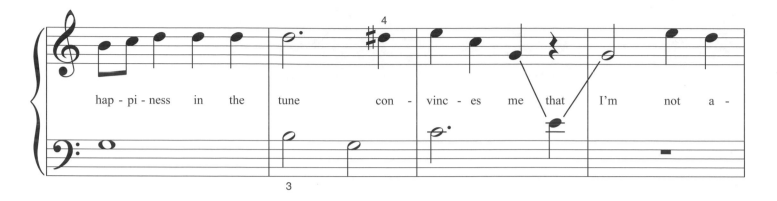

hap - pi - ness in the tune con - vinc - es me that I'm not a -

fraid. Make be - lieve you're

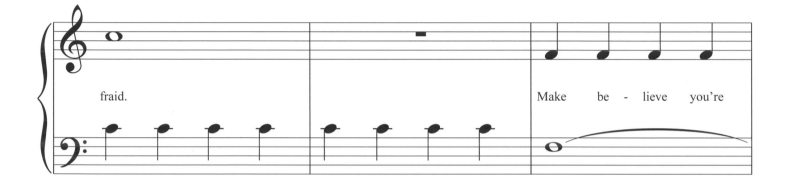

brave and the trick will take you far. You may be as

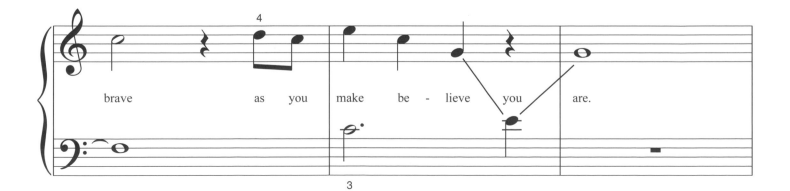

brave as you make be - lieve you are.

(Whistle)

You may be as brave

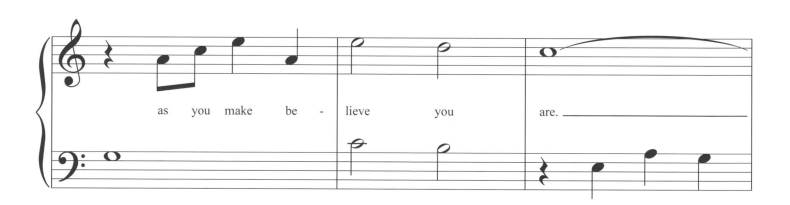

as you make be - lieve you are.

WAVING THROUGH A WINDOW
from DEAR EVAN HANSEN

Music and Lyrics by BENJ PASEK
and JUSTIN PAUL

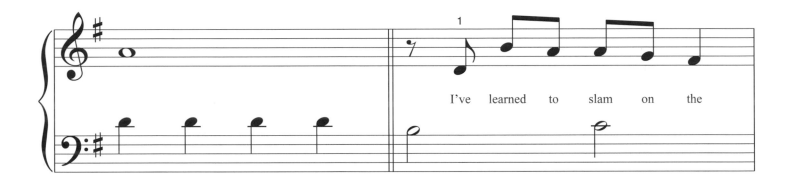

I've learned to slam on the

brake   be - fore I e - ven   turn the key

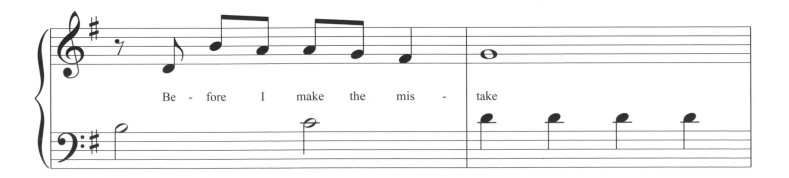

Be - fore I make the mis - take

Be - fore I lead with the worst of me ____

Give them no rea - son to stare

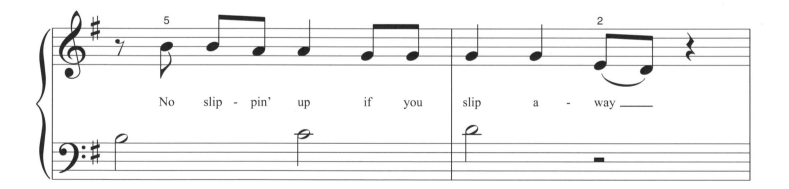

No slip - pin' up if you slip a - way ____

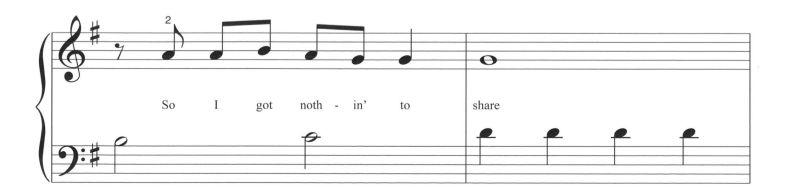

So I got noth - in' to share

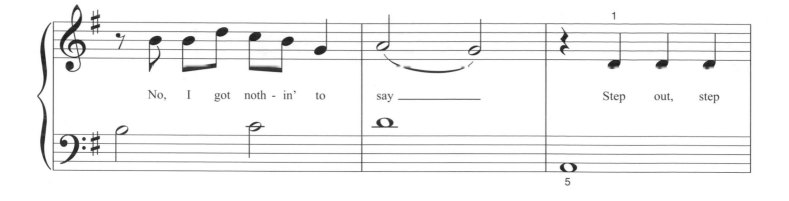

No, I got noth-in' to say ___ Step out, step

out - ta the sun if you keep get - tin' burned.

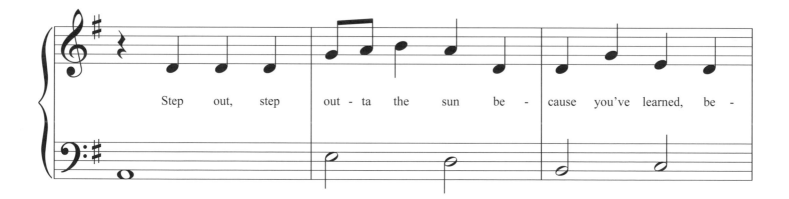

Step out, step out - ta the sun be - cause you've learned, be -

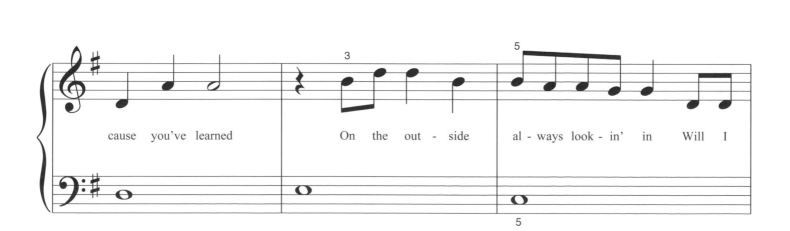

cause you've learned On the out - side al - ways look - in' in Will I

ev - er be more than I've al - ways been? 'Cause I'm tap - tap - tap - pin' on the

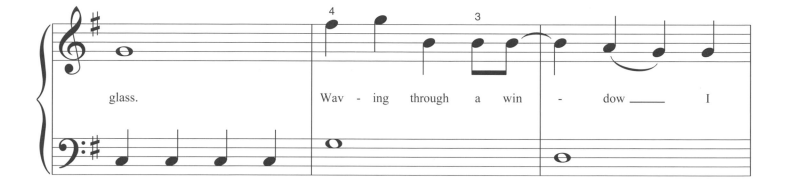

glass. Wav - ing through a win - dow _____ I

try to speak but no - bod - y can hear So I wait a - round for an

an - swer to ap - pear while I'm watch - watch - watch - in' peo - ple pass

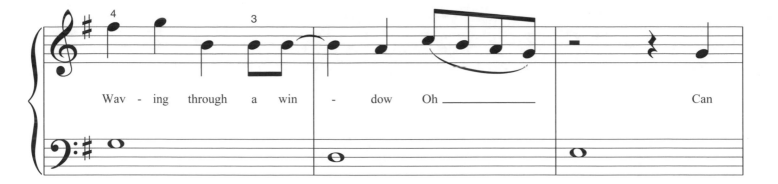

Wav - ing through a win - dow Oh _____ Can

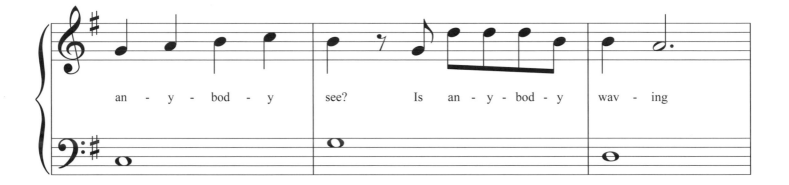

an - y - bod - y see? Is an - y - bod - y wav - ing

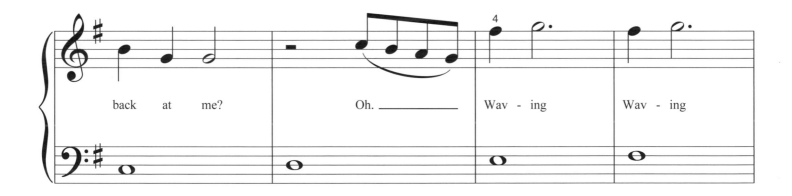

back at me? Oh. _____ Wav - ing Wav - ing

Whoa _____ whoa _____

Sunrise, Sunset

from the Musical FIDDLER ON THE ROOF

Words by SHELDON HARNICK
Music by JERRY BOCK

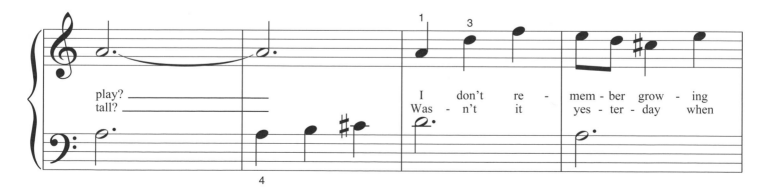

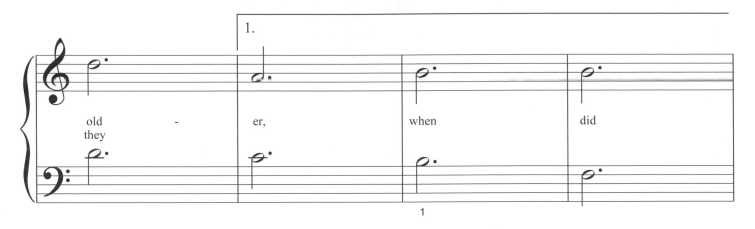

old -   er,   when   did
they

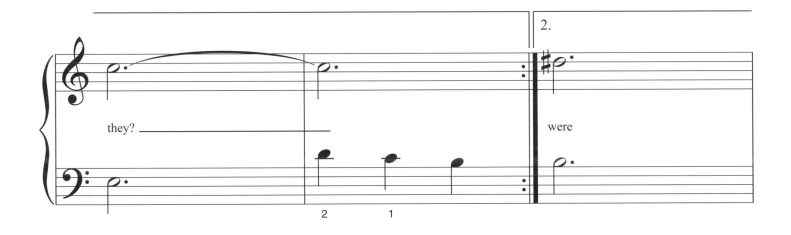

they? _____   were

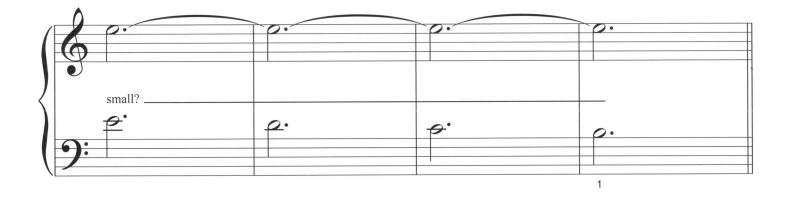

small? _____

Sun - rise, _____   sun - set,   sun - rise, _____
Sun - rise, _____   sun - set,   sun - rise, _____

sun - set, swift - ly flow the days;
sun - set, swift - ly fly the years;

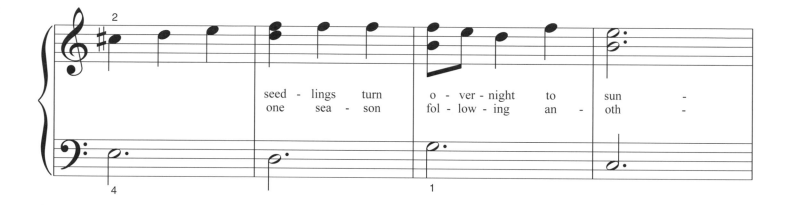

seed - lings turn o - ver - night to sun -
one sea - son fol - low - ing an - oth -

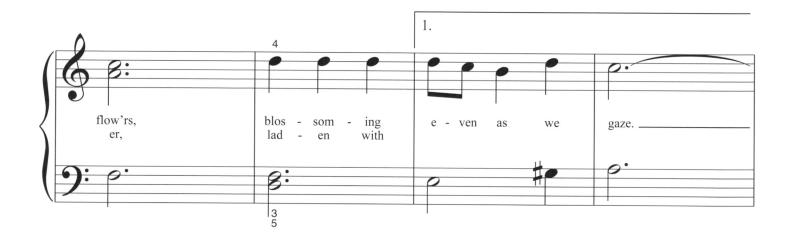

1.

flow'rs, blos - som - ing e - ven as we gaze.
er, lad - en with

2.

hap - pi - ness and tears.

TOMORROW
from the Musical Production ANNIE

Lyric by MARTIN CHARNIN
Music by CHARLES STROUSE

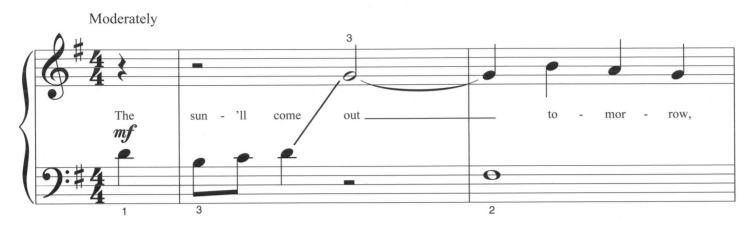

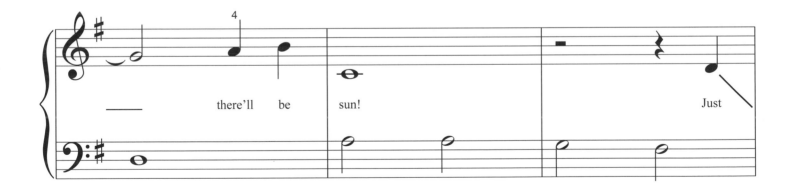

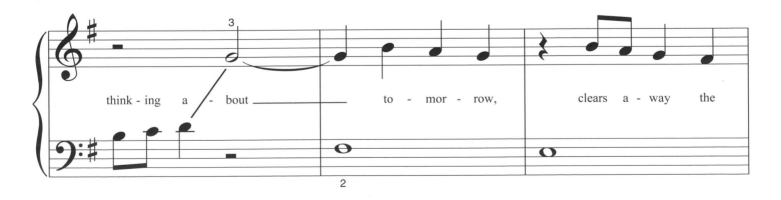

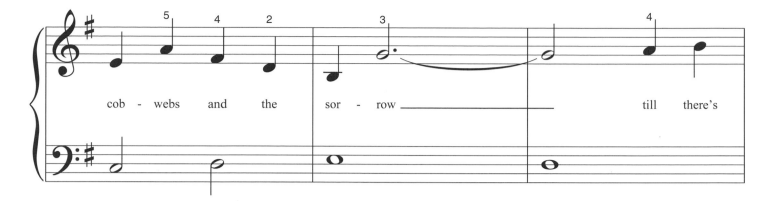

cob - webs and the sor - row _____ till there's

none. When I'm stuck with a day that's

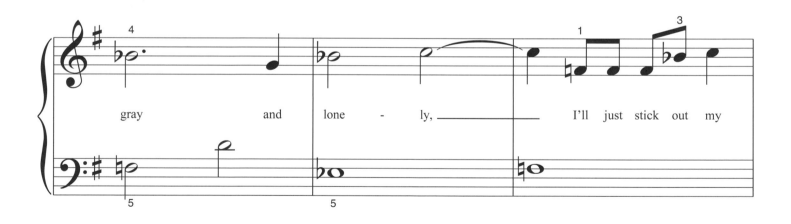

gray and lone - ly, _____ I'll just stick out my

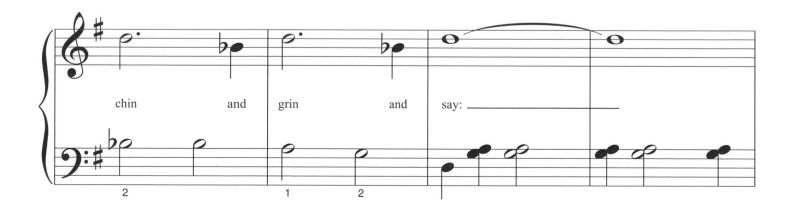

chin and grin and say: _____

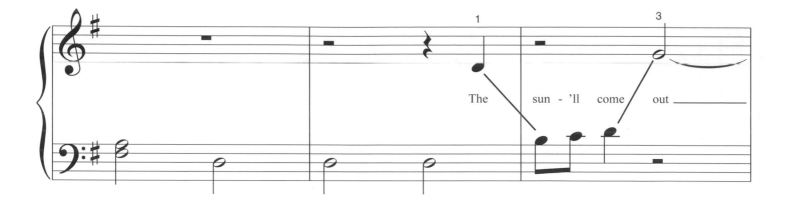

The sun - 'll come out ____

____ to - mor - row, so you got to hang on till to -

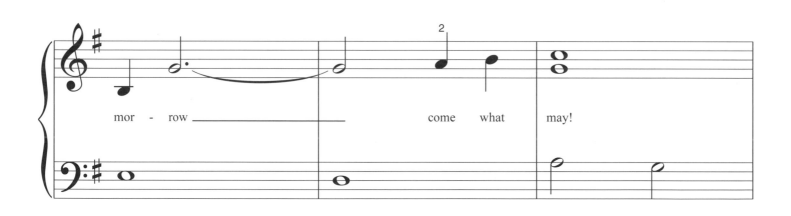

mor - row ____ come what may!

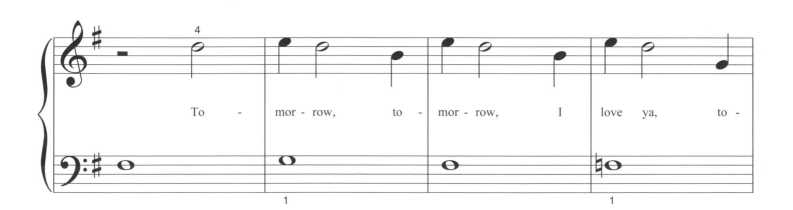

To - mor - row, to - mor - row, I love ya, to -

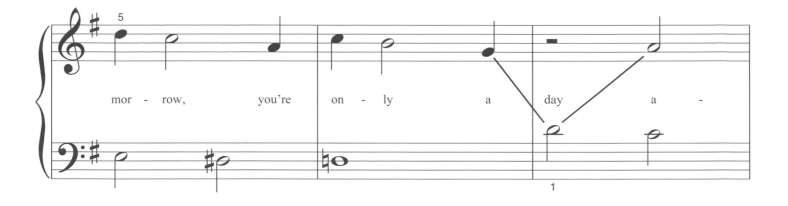

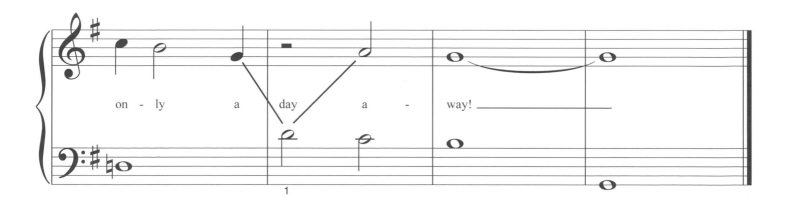

WHEN I GROW UP

from MATILDA THE MUSICAL

Words and Music by
TIM MINCHIN

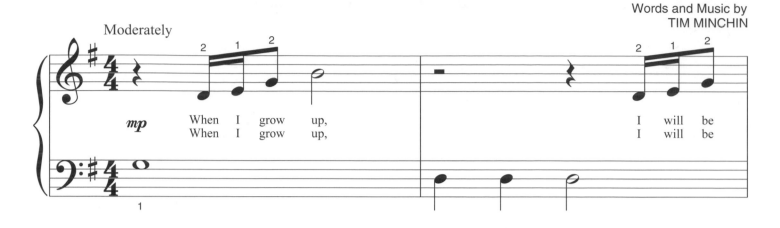

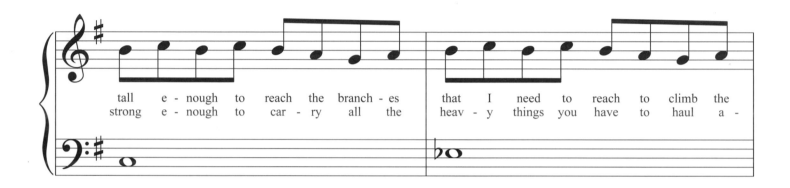

smart e - nough to an - swer all the ques - tions that you need to know the
brave e - nough to fight the crea - tures that you have to fight be - neath the

an - swers to be - fore you're grown up. _____
bed each night to be a grown - up. _____

And when I grow up I will eat sweets ev - 'ry day on the
And when I grow up I will have treats ev - 'ry day and I'll

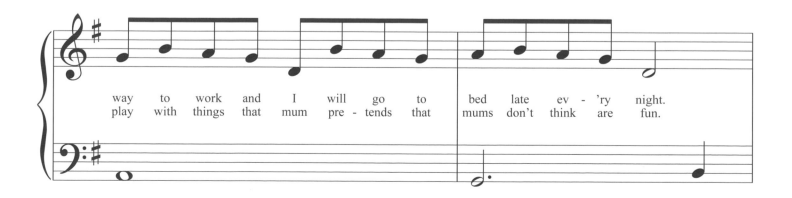

way to work and I will go to bed late ev - 'ry night.
play with things that mum pre - tends that mums don't think are fun.

And I will wake up when the sun comes up and I will watch car -
And I will wake up when the sun comes up and I will spend all

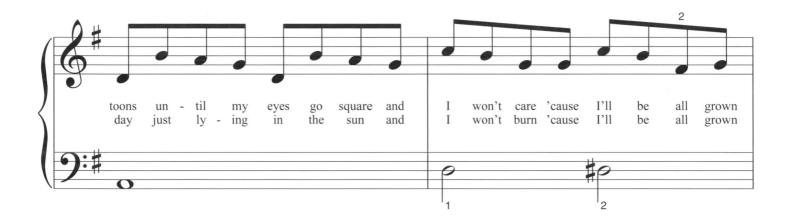

toons un – til my eyes go square and I won't care 'cause I'll be all grown
day just ly – ing in the sun and I won't burn 'cause I'll be all grown

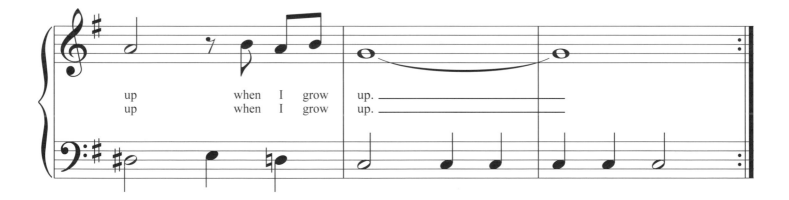

up   when I grow up. _____
up   when I grow up. _____

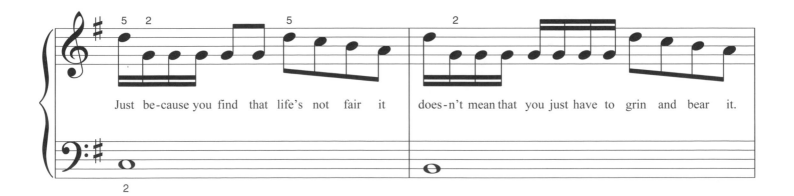

Just be-cause you find that life's not fair it   does-n't mean that you just have to grin and bear it.

If you al-ways take it on the chin and wear it noth-ing will change.

Just be-cause I find my-self in this sto-ry it does-n't mean that ev-'ry-thing is writ-ten for me.

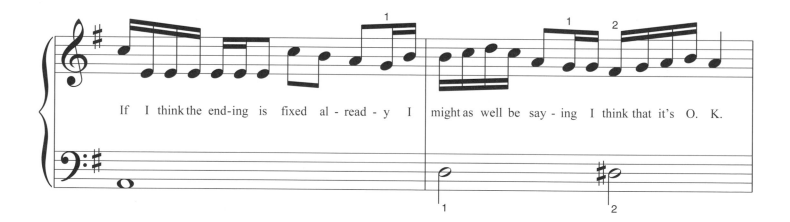

If I think the end-ing is fixed al-read-y I might as well be say-ing I think that it's O. K.

And that's not right!

mf

BEGINNING PIANO SOLO

Hal Leonard Beginning Piano Solos are created for students in the first and second years of study. These arrangements include a simple presentation of melody and harmony for a first "solo" experience. See www.halleonard.com for complete song lists.

00153652 The Charlie Brown Collection™.....$10.99

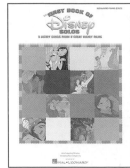
00316058 First Book of Disney Solos $12.99

00311065 Jazz Standards $9.95

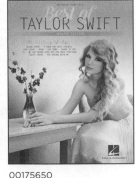
00103239 The Phantom of the Opera.....................$12.99

00175650 Best of Taylor Swift...$12.99

00156395 Adele $12.99

00311063 Classical Favorites $8.99

00130375 Frozen.......$12.99

00118420 Best of Carole King ...$10.99

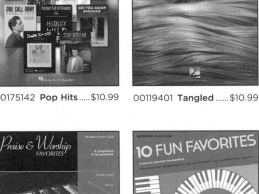
00175142 Pop Hits $10.99

00119401 Tangled $10.99

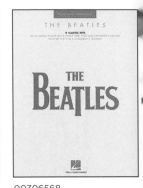
00306568 The Beatles $12.99

00316082 Contemporary Disney Solos $12.99

00311799 Gospel Hymn Favorites$8.99

00103351 Les Misérables $12.99

00311271 Praise & Worship Favorites $9.95

00110390 10 Fun Favorites $9.99

00307153 Songs of the Beatles $9.99

00311431 Disney Classics $10.99

00311064 Greatest Pop Hits.........$9.99

00319465 The Lion King $12.99

00316037 The Sound of Music ...$10.99

00109365 Wicked $10.99

00279152 Cartoon Favorites $9.99

00264691 Disney Hits $10.99

00319418 It's a Beautiful Day with Mr. Rogers....$8.99

00110402 The Most Beautiful Songs Ever $14.99

00110287 Star Wars ..$12.99

00194545 John Williams...............$10.99

HAL•LEONARD®
www.halleonard.com

Prices, contents and availability are subject to change without notice. Disney characters and artwork TM & © 2019 Disney